AF584453

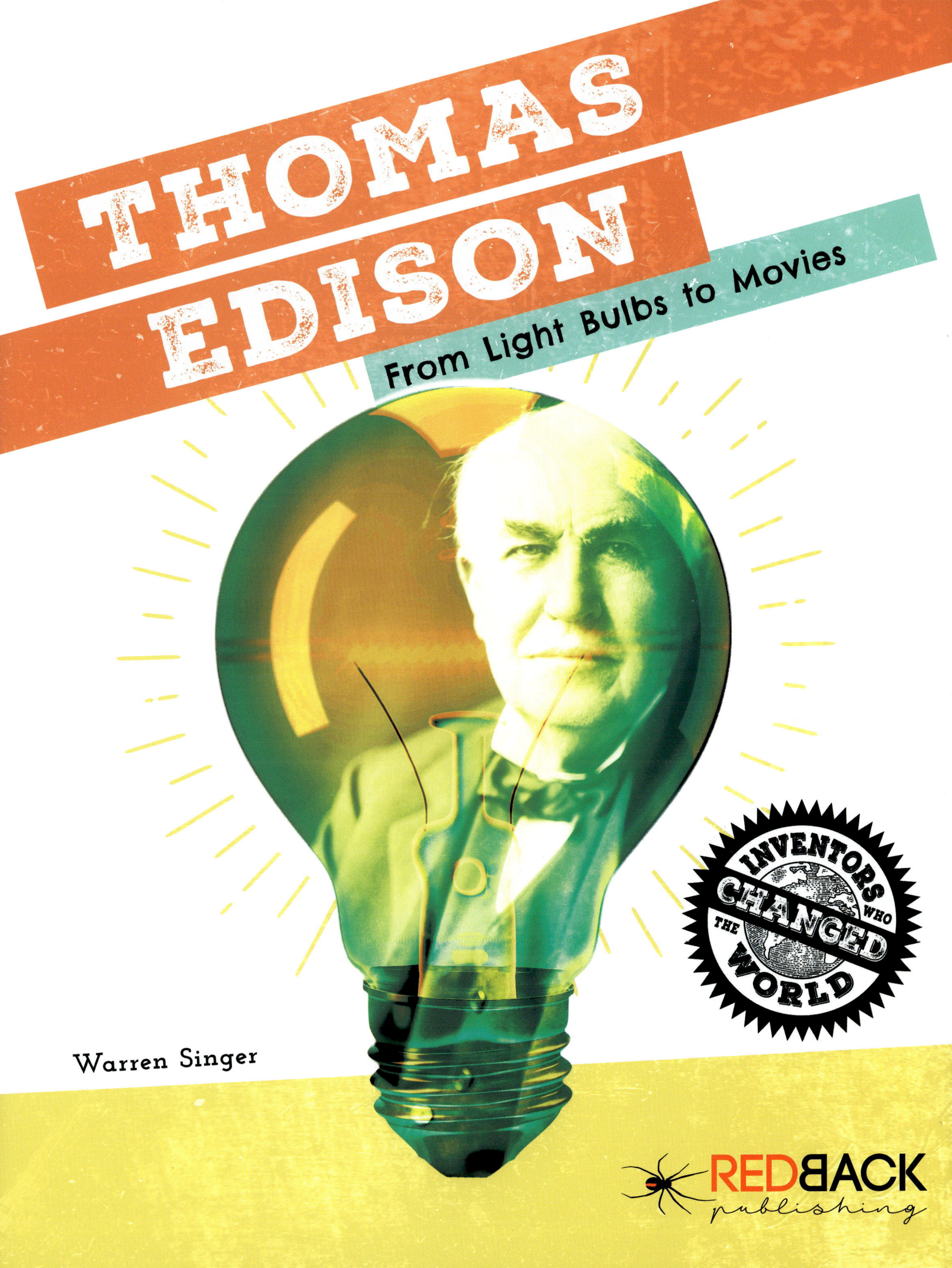
THOMAS EDISON
From Light Bulbs to Movies
INVENTORS WHO CHANGED THE WORLD
Warren Singer
REDBACK publishing

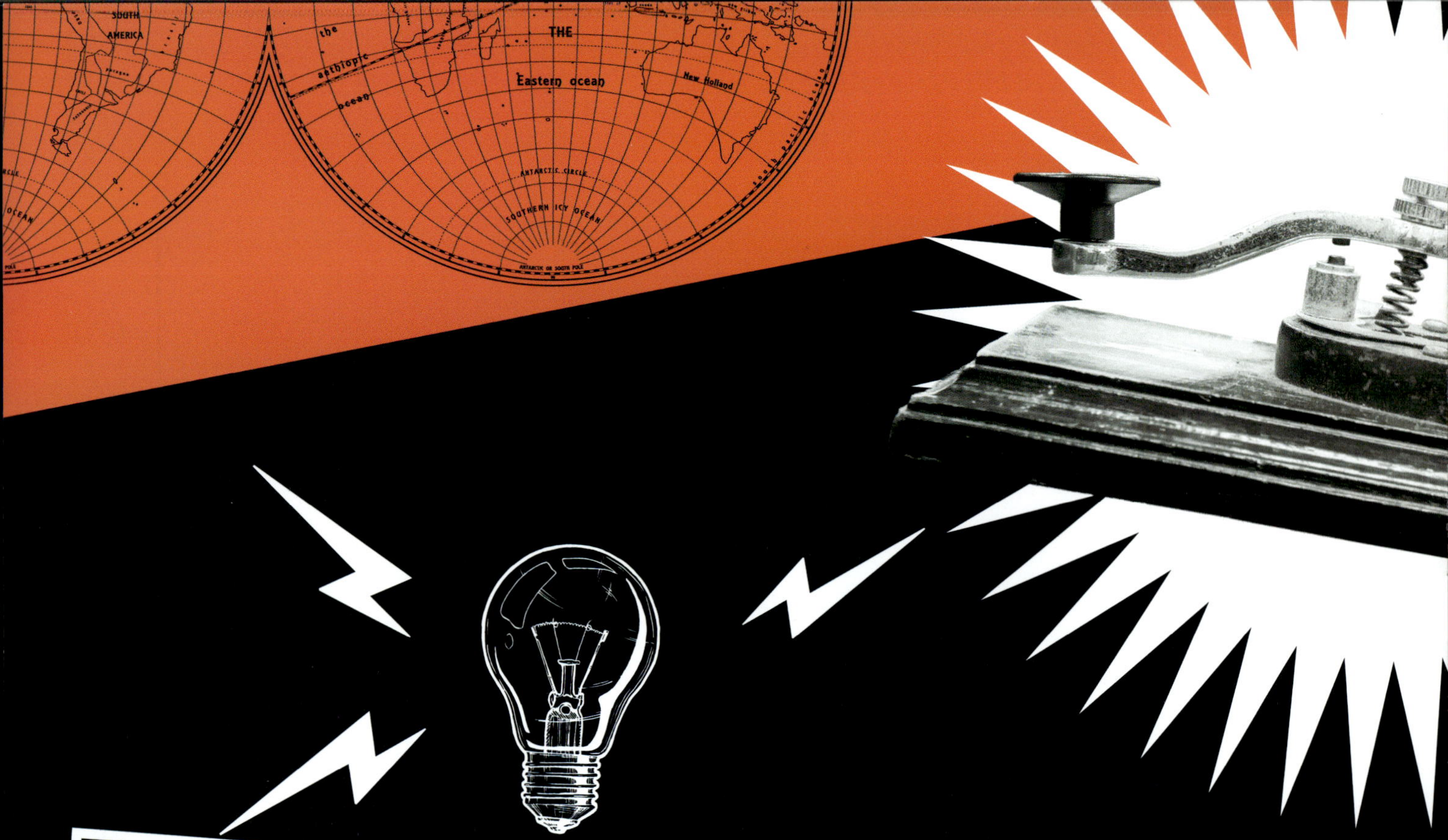

First Published 2026
Redback Publishing
Suite 6, 13a Narabang Way,
Belrose NSW 2085
Australia

www.redbackpublishing.com
orders@redbackpublishing.com

ISBN 978-1-761402-06-7

Author: Warren Singer
Editors: Lucinda Dodds and Emma Dobinson
Design: Redback Publishing

Original illustrations © Redback Publishing 2026
Originated by Redback Publishing

A catalogue record for this book is available from the National Library of Australia

Acknowledgements
Abbreviations: l—left, r—right, b—bottom, t—top, c—centre, m—middle
We would like to thank the following for permission to reproduce photographs: (Images © shutterstock)
P4tr Dennis MacDonald / Shutterstock.com, p8b claudio zaccherini / Shutterstock.com, p10ml General Electric, Public domain, via Wikimedia Commons, p11br H.C. White Co., Public domain, via Wikimedia Commons, p12b James R. Martin / Shutterstock.com, p13ml Dennis MacDonald / Shutterstock.com, p14m English: NPGallery, Public domain, via Wikimedia Commons, p15mr English: NPGallery, Public domain, via Wikimedia Commons, p16br Anonymous, Public domain, via Wikimedia Commons, p17tl Created by Thomas A. Edison Studios, Inc. (New Jersey) for publication(Life time: Published for defunct corporation by defunct trade journal prior to 1926), Public domain, via Wikimedia Commons, p17br Mabalu, CC BY-SA 4.0 <https://creativecommons.org/licenses/by-sa/4.0>, via Wikimedia Commons, p19tr Photo Spirit / Shutterstock.com, p21tl SunflowerMomma / Shutterstock.com, p21ml Science Museum Group Collection, p22b 4kclips / Shutterstock.com, p24tr Edison, Thomas A. (Thomas Alva), 1847-1931;Peters, N. (Norris), lithographer;Hammer, William Joseph, 1858-1934, former owner. DSI;Edison, Thomas A. (Thomas Alva), 1847-1931, inscriber. DSI;United States. Patent Office, No restrictions, via Wikimedia Commons, p26mr EQRoy / Shutterstock.com, p26m AMaken, CC BY 4.0 <https://creativecommons.org/licenses/by/4.0>, via Wikimedia Commons, p27t English: NPGallery, Public domain, via Wikimedia Commons, pg27b English: NPGallery, Public domain, via Wikimedia Commons, p29tl Thomas Edison (reprinted by the Norris Peters Co.), Public domain, via Wikimedia Commons, pg29mr National Archives at College Park - Cartographic, Public domain, via Wikimedia Commons, pg30m Ritu Manoj Jethani / Shutterstock.com, pg31m National Park Service / Thomas Edison National Historical Park, Public domain, via Wikimedia Commons, p31br Carsten Reisinger / Shutterstock.com

CONTENTS

HOME-SCHOOLED INVENTOR

Thomas Edison is America's most famous inventor, but he spent only a few months at school.

HOME-SCHOOLED

Thomas Alva Edison was born on 11 February 1847, in Ohio, USA. He did not do well at school, so his mother, who was a school teacher, decided to teach him herself at home.

Encouraged to read and explore, Edison developed an intense interest in the use of electricity, doing chemistry experiments and even thinking about novel ways of setting up businesses.

GENIUS

Although he is now widely honoured as one of the most important Americans who has ever lived, Edison's genius caused him some problems as a child and young man. For example, when he was only 12 years old, Edison worked selling newspapers on a train and he spent his spare time doing chemistry experiments between train trips. He lost that job when one of the experiments resulted in a damaging fire on a train.

DEAFNESS

Edison became almost deaf when he was a child. Rather than giving up on his dreams and interest in inventing, he pushed himself to read and learn more, so that having a disability would not be a disadvantage for achieving what he felt driven to do.

HONOURED

Edison died in 1931 at the age of 84. He was thinking about new inventions almost until the very end of his life. The boy who had not done well at school ended up being honoured by President Hoover, who asked every American to turn off their electric light bulbs for one minute to show their sadness for the loss of the country's greatest inventor.

IMPROVING THE TELEGRAPH

Working for a number of telegraph businesses gave Edison useful knowledge about the way the telegraph system operated.

TELEGRAPH OPERATOR

When he was 15, one of Edison's jobs was working as a telegraph operator. This fascinated him and gave him the background knowledge he needed to later invent a better way of sending telegraph messages.

MORSE CODE

Before telephones and satellites, the telegraph was the only way to send and receive long-distance messages. The messages were sent over wires using a pattern of clicks for dots and dashes, forming an alphabetic Morse code.

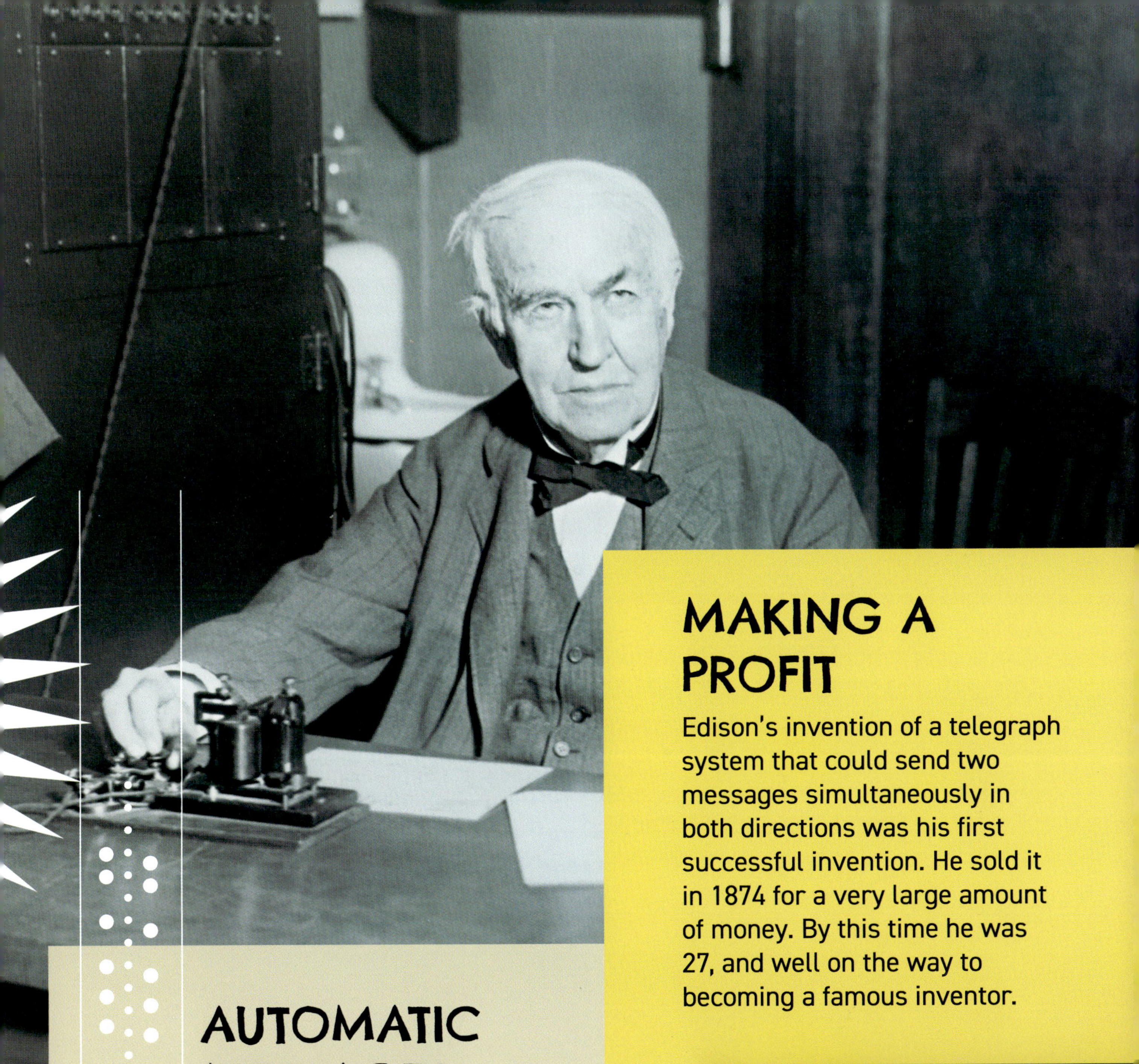

MAKING A PROFIT

Edison's invention of a telegraph system that could send two messages simultaneously in both directions was his first successful invention. He sold it in 1874 for a very large amount of money. By this time he was 27, and well on the way to becoming a famous inventor.

AUTOMATIC MESSAGES

Edison also invented a way to send automatic telegraph messages by preparing rolls of paper punched with holes to represent the dots and dashes of Morse code. The paper roll ran through a machine that converted the holes into an electronic message.

LIGHT BULB

Did Edison really invent the light bulb?

LIGHTING

Without doubt, Edison's most famous invention was making improvements to the electric light bulb. Before this invention, lighting at night was made by the use of candles and oil lamps or the burning of gas. The light bulb changed society by extending work and study hours and it also changed the way people relaxed in the evenings.

TESTING, TESTING ...

Edison began thinking about a design for an improved light bulb in the late 1870s. Light bulbs had already been invented, but they were impractical, lasted a short time and were very expensive. Edison and his team tested many substances for the filament in the bulb that would produce the most amount of light for the longest time. His team discovered that a filament of bamboo, when burned into carbon, would emit light for over 1,000 hours.

FINAL DESIGN

Edison's final design made light bulbs cheaper and more reliable, and this meant that ordinary people could afford to buy them. His aim was to make the use of electricity and technological devices that used electricity cheap enough for the majority of people to have electricity in their homes and businesses.

SOLD TO THE WORLD

Edison's light bulbs were eventually used in other parts of the world, making his invention a worldwide phenomenon.

ELECTRICITY TO THE PEOPLE

In the late 1800s, electricity was the new power source that everyone was talking about.

COMPETING WITH GAS

Edison realised that just manufacturing a new light bulb, or any other piece of technology that used electricity, was not enough. He needed to be in competition with the gas companies that had, until then, been the main providers of lighting.

COMPETING WITH OTHER INVENTORS

In the 1880s, Edison set up an electricity distribution business, which used steam power to generate an electric current that could be sent to homes and businesses.

Many businesses wanted to be the suppliers of the electric power that would be needed to run all the new devices that were being invented, so he faced much competition in this venture.

BUSINESS WIZARD

Edison was not only a scientist and inventor. He was also a businessman.

GROUP OF EXPERTS

Rather than working alone to create his new inventions, Edison developed the idea that inventing could be done by groups of experts working together in a business. This is the way that most modern inventions are developed today, and it has resulted in the new technology we use in computers, mobile phones and digital technology equipment.

NEW WAY OF OPERATING

Before Edison's business approach to inventing, many inventors worked alone or in small teams. They were either scientists or engineers who worked at universities, or they were wealthy people who could spend their time inventing, without the need to earn a living from their work.

WIZARD OF MENLO PARK

Edison was 29 when he opened his own research laboratory and factory at Menlo Park in New Jersey, USA. The inventions that came out of this industrial complex were so amazing that Edison earned the nickname 'The Wizard of Menlo Park'.

His success led to him establishing a larger laboratory at West Orange, New Jersey. Today, his facilities would be called Research and Development (R&D) labs.

MOVIES

Photography was a new art form when Edison started work on how to make moving pictures.

FILM

In the 1890s, Edison and his team experimented with placing images on a strip of film. They then designed a machine to make the strip move at a constant speed. This produced the illusion of a moving picture. Until digital photography began being used in the 1990s, Edison's idea of using a strip of film continued to be the way that moving pictures, or movies, were made.

FIRST FILM PRODUCTION

Edison and his inventors designed a film camera, called a Kinetograph, and a machine called a Kinetoscope, which showed these mini movies by running the film strip over a light source.

FILM STUDIO

In 1893, Edison opened the first film studio in the world in New Jersey. He produced films there. His first film was shown to the public in 1894, but it was not shown on a screen. Instead, people paid to view the short film through a peephole in the Kinetoscope.

MOVIE INDUSTRY

Edison's work with film strips formed the basis of the movie industry which later developed in the USA. His filmmaking ideas were soon copied and developed in other countries, with France being the first country where a film on a large screen was shown to the public.

PHONOGRAPH

Edison's first recordings of the human voice shocked and amazed the public.

FOR HOME USE

Edison invented the phonograph in 1877. During the late 1800s, Edison further developed the phonograph for home use. Sound was recorded on a cylinder, then played back by turning a handle. People could record themselves speaking or buy music cylinders. This was the first time that people could hear their favourite songs being played in their own homes.

12 THE MOTION PICTURE NEWS

EDISON

**THE ADVENTURE OF THE STOLEN SLIPPER
Fourth "Octavius" Story
Starring BARRY O'MOORE

Our toy detective rushes to the rescue of a fair damsel, blunders upon a real crook, and gets his face slapped for trying to reform the girl.

"Pictorial Review" will help you feature this series

This film released Monday, April 20th

**THE MYSTERY OF THE SILVER SNARE
Sixth "Cleek" Story
Featuring BEN WILSON

The most sensational of the Cleek stories thus far shows the great detective trapped by a gang of Apaches.

Ask "Short Stories" for its advertising helps and its co-operation in showing this big detective series.

This film released Tuesday, April 28th

Coming Two Reel Features

***FREDERICK THE GREAT — Friday, May 1st
A drama of his life.

***THE SONG OF SOLOMON — Friday, May 8th
Comedy-Drama.

Coming Single Reels

**HER GRANDMOTHER'S WEDDING DRESS — Saturday, May 2nd
Drama.

*A WEEK-END AT HAPPYHURST — Monday, May 4th
Comedy.

**THE DOUBLE CROSS — Tuesday, May 5th
Third "The Man Who Disappeared."

*THE LUCKY VEST — Wednesday, May 6th
Comedy.

**THE END OF THE UMBRELLA — Saturday, May 9th
Seventh "Dolly" story.

*MARTHA'S REBELLION — Monday, May 11th
Comedy.

*AN ALASKAN INTERLUDE — Tuesday, May 12th
Drama.

***ANDY PLAYS CUPID — Wednesday, May 13th
Sixth "Andy" story.

*One sheets. **One and three sheets. ***One, three and six sheet posters by the Morgan Lithograph Co.

TRADE MARK
Thomas A Edison
Makers of the Edison Kinetoscope, Model "D."

THOMAS A. EDISON, Inc.
275 Lakeside Avenue
Orange, N. J.

In writing to advertisers please mention "THE MOTION PICTURE NEWS"

TALKING MOVIES

Edison invented the Kinetophone as a way of adding sound to his movies, but he found it difficult to make the sound and action work together perfectly. One of the outcomes was that silent movies were all that was available until the 1920s.

DOLLS

Constantly thinking of new ways to use every invention, Edison was also the first to market dolls that could talk. They were made available for sale in 1890 and had a phonograph cylinder inside them.

PASSION FOR CHEMISTRY

Doing chemical experiments had been one of Edison's passions from a very early age.

CHEMISTRY COURSE

Edison's desire to discover the details of chemistry continued throughout his life. Doing a chemistry course at a college was one of the rare times that he looked to formal education to give him the answers he needed.

CHEMICAL STOREHOUSE

Edison's factory and laboratories had their own stores of every sort of chemical that the inventors might have needed. This sped up the design process, contributing to Edison's inventing success.

PHENOL C_6H_6O

Producing phenol was a very profitable business for Edison. Phenol was used to manufacture his phonograph recordings, but it was also used for making aspirin and explosives.

RUBBER

Testing hundreds of plants that could be a new source of rubber was an activity that interested Edison in the 1920s, during the last years of his life. America had experienced shortages of rubber during the First World War, and Edison believed a more reliable, local source would be better than relying on imports.

MICROPHONE

Edison's design for a telephone microphone was used in telephones around the world for decades.

BEING THE FIRST

In the late 1800s, the international drive to be the first to produce inventions using electricity led to many court cases about who was the first to invent a new piece of technology. An example of this involved Edison's improvements to the telephone microphone.

Emile Berliner and Thomas Edison battled in court for the right to be known as the inventor of the carbon button microphone, with Edison winning the case.

CARBON BUTTON MICROPHONE

Before Edison's invention of the carbon button microphone in the 1870s, the sound you could hear over a telephone receiver was faint and difficult to understand.

HOW IT WORKED

A carbon button is placed in a telephone mouthpiece, between metal plates that conduct electricity. This results in the sound waves being converted into an electric current. This invention was used right up until the 1980s.

The sound was so good that early telephones using the new carbon button were called the 'Edison Loud-Speaking Telephone'.

CEMENT

Building materials are not normally at the top of the list when we are thinking about the inventions of Thomas Edison.

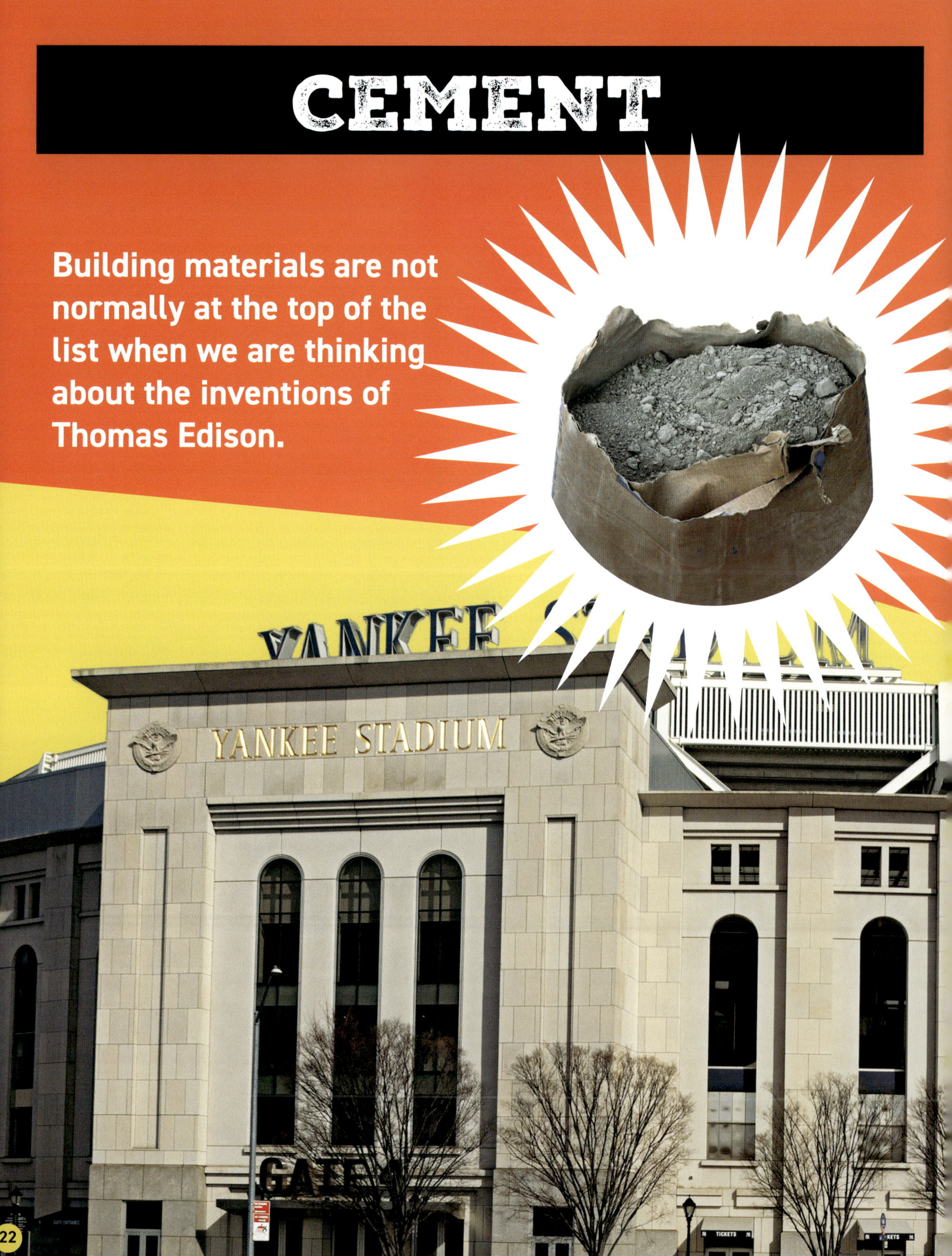

SAND AND CEMENT

Edison worked on a better way to produce iron ore. This produced a lot of sand, which cement makers were keen to buy from him. In his usual way, Edison invented a better way to use this sand to make a much stronger cement.

CEMENT HOUSES

Edison was always thinking of different ways to use his inventions. One of these was his plan to make houses cheaper by building them entirely out of cement. Although this was not one of his best businesses, it is an idea that is widely used today in factory construction, and in prefabrication of building walls.

YANKEE STADIUM

The famous Yankee Stadium in New York used Edison's cement in its construction. Many parts of the cement structures were so strong that renovators in the 1970s did not need to replace them.

ELECTRIC PEN

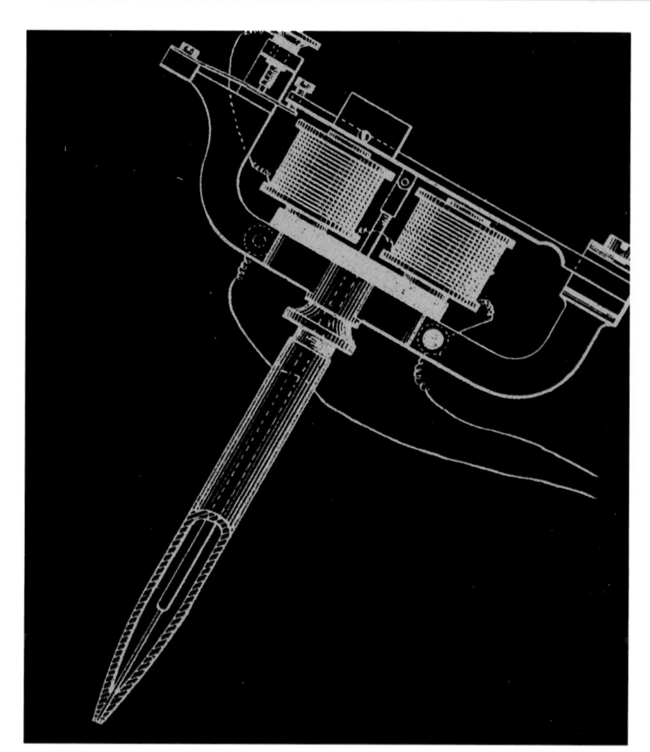

The electric pen sounds like it would have to be a modern, digital invention, but Edison designed one back in 1875.

COPYING A DOCUMENT

Edison designed his inventions so they would attract the interest of both people at home and businesses. The electronic pen was aimed at making it easier for a business to make copies of a document.

MAKING A STENCIL

Inside the device was an electric motor attached to a pen tip. As the user wrote, the tip made holes in a sheet of paper, resulting in a stencil that could be used for printing. The stencil could be placed on a press, ink was spread on top, then used to make printed copies. The electric pen became popular around the world.

TATTOOS

A surprising use for the electric pen idea was when another inventor used the technology to make an electric tattoo needle.

WORKING TOGETHER

Edison was a pioneer in his use of teamwork to produce the fastest results in the creation of new inventions.

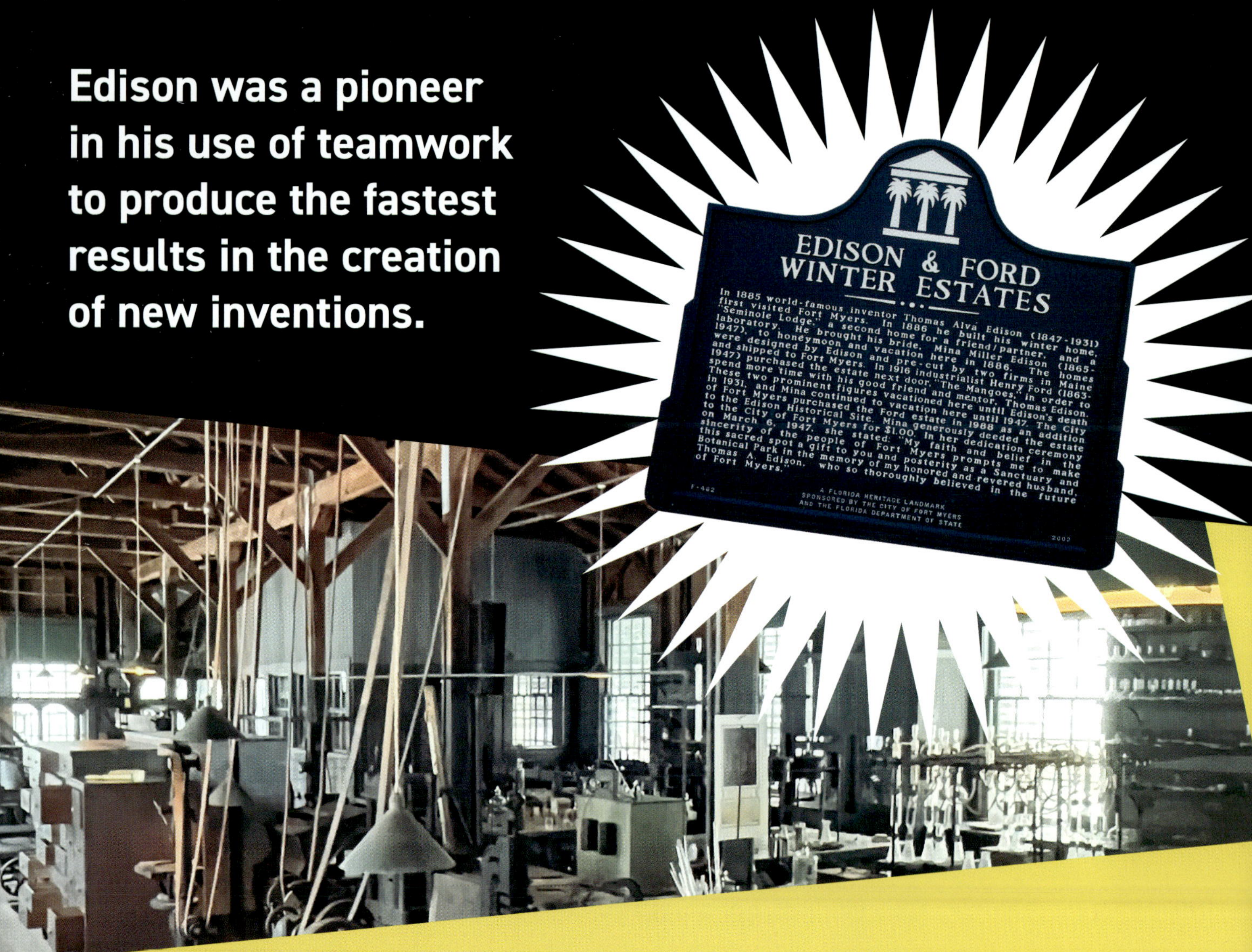

RESEARCH AND DEVELOPMENT

Gathering together a team of experts to solve problems and come up with new ideas is called Research and Development or R&D today.

Edison used this method in his industrial complexes. It is one of the reasons he was able to produce so many new inventions in his lifetime.

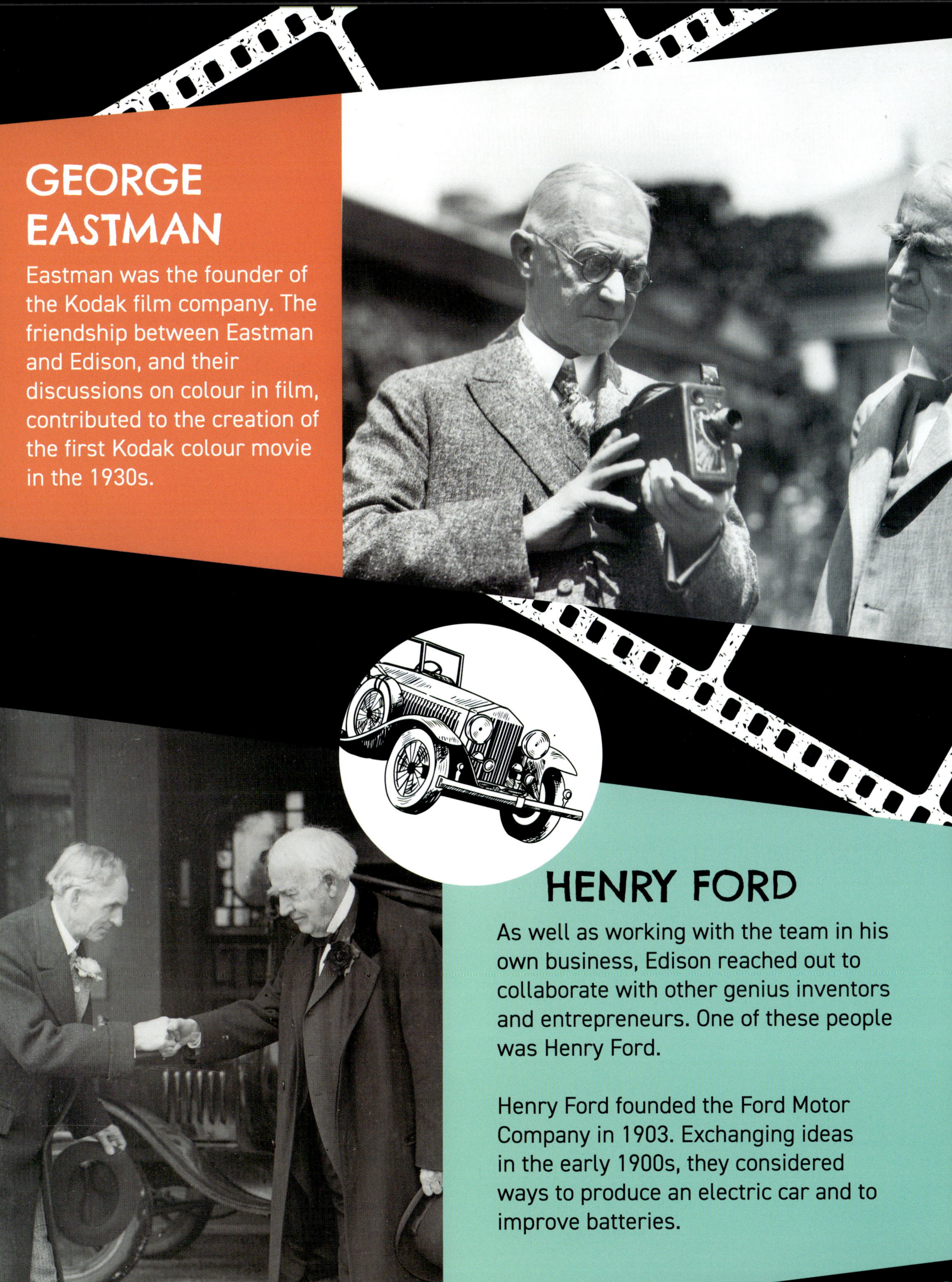

GEORGE EASTMAN

Eastman was the founder of the Kodak film company. The friendship between Eastman and Edison, and their discussions on colour in film, contributed to the creation of the first Kodak colour movie in the 1930s.

HENRY FORD

As well as working with the team in his own business, Edison reached out to collaborate with other genius inventors and entrepreneurs. One of these people was Henry Ford.

Henry Ford founded the Ford Motor Company in 1903. Exchanging ideas in the early 1900s, they considered ways to produce an electric car and to improve batteries.

PATENTS

Edison obtained over a thousand patents for his inventions during his lifetime.

WHAT IS A PATENT?

A patent is a government issued right to claim that an invention is owned by a person. It confirms that the patent owner can make and sell an invention. A patent usually only applies in the country in which it is issued. This means than an inventor needs to apply for patents in different countries to stop people there making and selling the technology.

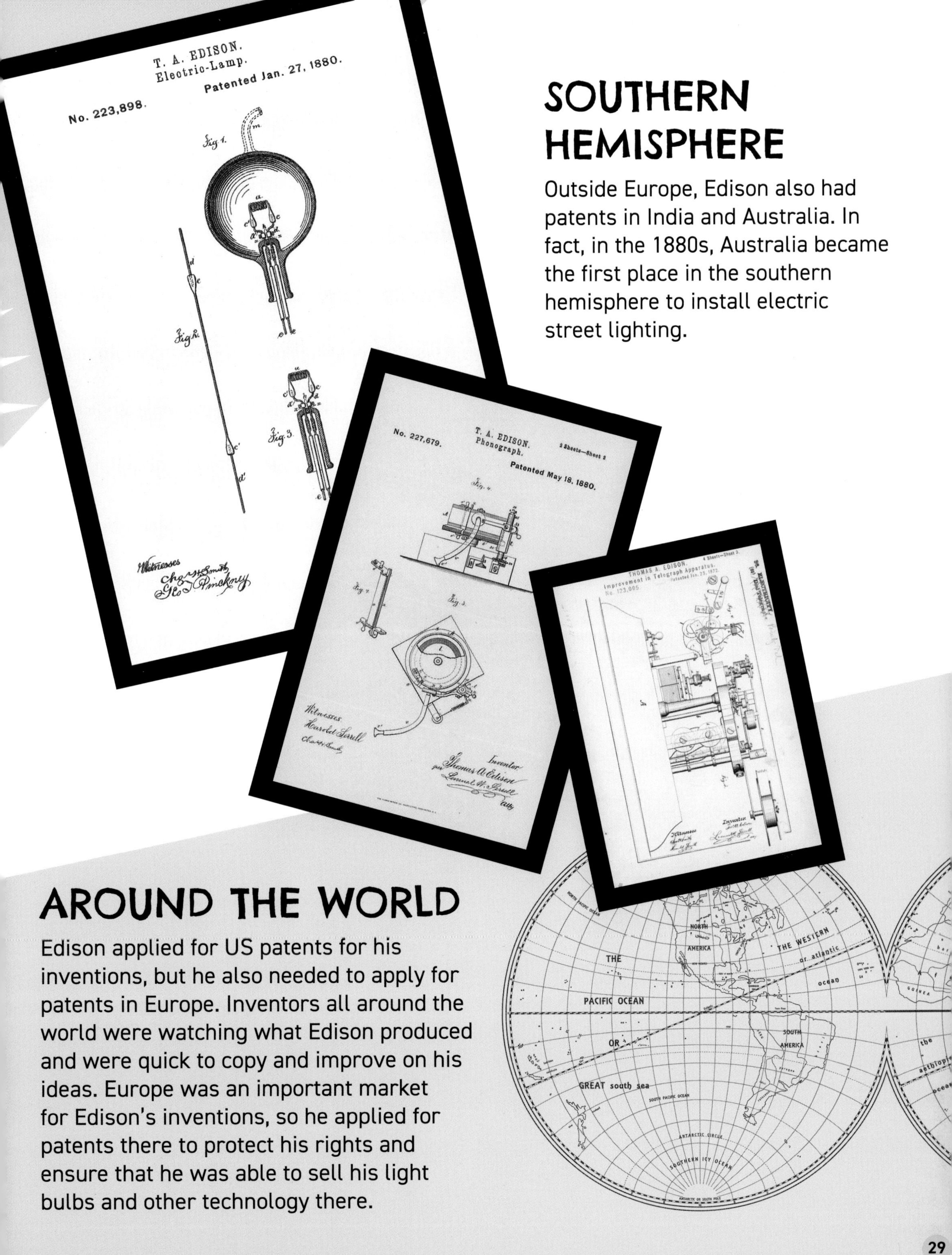

SOUTHERN HEMISPHERE

Outside Europe, Edison also had patents in India and Australia. In fact, in the 1880s, Australia became the first place in the southern hemisphere to install electric street lighting.

AROUND THE WORLD

Edison applied for US patents for his inventions, but he also needed to apply for patents in Europe. Inventors all around the world were watching what Edison produced and were quick to copy and improve on his ideas. Europe was an important market for Edison's inventions, so he applied for patents there to protect his rights and ensure that he was able to sell his light bulbs and other technology there.

FAMOUS

Edison's fame was due to a combination of his genius, his business skill and his practical approach to science.

TEAMWORK

Edison gathered around him a team of experts in science, engineering and technology. He gave them the ideas to work on, or they produced their own, and the whole team then came together to produce results.

If they needed machine parts that did not exist, Edison's own factory made them to suit the needs of the inventors. If one of his ideas involved specialist knowledge that Edison did not have, there would always be a team member at his factory who could step in and provide the information needed.

SETTING A STANDARD

Edison was a very practical inventor, making new technology that became familiar to people everywhere during his own lifetime. His revolutionary way of inventing and creating new technology set a standard that was followed by others everywhere. Many of Edison's inventions were the basis of technologies we all use today.

GENERAL ELECTRIC

Edison was one of the founders of the business that became known as General Electric, a household name around the world for many years.

GLOSSARY

cylinder tube that is flat at both ends
emit give out
entrepreneur person who is good at starting new businesses
filament part of a light bulb that glows
mouthpiece part of an old telephone into which a person spoke
phenomenon amazing thing or event
prefabrication making items in a factory rather than on a building site
telegraph long distance communication method using Morse code
venture activity to produce a special result

INDEX